Days on Planet

Jeff Marple

Prairie Muse Books

2024

Contents

Hitler was a
Spiritual Man

I've never had a gun
  put to my head
Never had family make advances
  in bed
Never had drunks posing
  as parents
I have a pretty good life
  it's becoming apparent

and I've never had to sell my
  body for food
or steal a warm coat so as not
  to turn blue
I've never been hungry for
  more than an hour
Always hot water when I
  take a shower

No I've never been marked
   by these trials and abuses
So why are my good intentions
   tied down by excuses?

Hitler had his chances to be a
    good man
Just like Martin Luther and
    the Son of Sam
and Mother Teresa
and the neighbor next door
and the man sleeping in vomit
    on his cold bathroom floor

and the sexy supermodel
the man sizing your shoes
and the popes and the pimps
    and the me and the you

Earthquakes and tsunamis rage
    out of control
A slave to their nature not
    divine moral code
But I must come with
    suggestions etched with care
    on my soul
and I can take them
    or leave them
but they won't leave me alone

Brothers

It's easy to be patriotic
watching the parade
   on the porch
with a gin and tonic

But what I've read
about soldiers up front,
a military parade is the last
   thing they'd want

First they want to be
   a brother
Just do their job
Protect each other
No falling confetti or
   waving flags
Just keep each other out of
   body bags

To live, just one day older
Taste their mother's cake
squeeze their girlfriend's
   shoulder
or read a magazine
   out in a hammock
all these things we take
   for granted

But their feet are wet
and their tongues are dry
Dodging melting metal
under burning sky

But this is just
   what I have read
I've never smelled the stench
   of death

So crumple these words and
   throw them away
then go look into a combat
   soldier's face
Take the stare in his eyes
   with you to bed
They tell much more than what I
   have said

Securely Insane

Yet again I'm asked
    the last four of my soshe
I don't like that word - it's
    like a combination of
    douche and soap
It's a soft squishy sound
    it's not even a word
but I say it right back
    which is even more absurd

What's with this particular
    abbreviation I wonder
Can't we all just call it
    a social security number?
Perhaps not, and that's what's
    giving me a fit
I've said my last four so much
    I don't know my first six

But I've memorized my passwords
    - all 25
I just can't remember
    to which sites they apply
Disturbing new words I've had
    to make up
Because they keep making me
    change my fucking passwords
        so much
Schizocyberphrenia - that's my
    self-diagnosis
Because aren't neologisms
    the first sign of psychosis?

So I called the clinic
    emergency line
and they put me on hold
    which they do all the time
Then I get automated numerical
    options
"Press 9 if you feel like
    poking your eyes out"
        is the one I press
            most often.

That's why I don't see what's
    so bad about identity theft
Let someone else have the
    crisis when my sanity
        has left.

T.L. The Destroyer

My insecurity machine
    barely functions
Crushed in the path of
    True Love's destruction
And those stipulations
Itemized then bolted down
    in neat rows
lay battered and lifeless
    all over the road

I held my worries
    in a vice grip
knuckled tight in
    my clenched fists
But True Love's fury is
    vengeful and seething
Now they're twisted and bent
in a ditch barely breathing

My love is plywood
It splinters then scatters
A porcelain plate
It flies when it shatters

Another cruel casualty of
     True Love's great wrath
But if you ever see it coming
I suggest you stand in its path

Late Service

I don't favor church much
I've a parade of excuses
the offering plate and the
   priest abuses
The smiling jesus machines
wearing slacks
I'm in jeans

But I went to a late service
Lost a bet with a friend
Sat in the back by the aisle
for a quick escape when it ends.

The opening hymn was
   histrionic and shrill
I couldn't sing that high
   at the top of a hill
So I lip synced and looked
around in the pews
and realized right then that I
   recognized a few...

The man from the grocery
the one who stacks cans
he's recently divorced and just
    out of rehab
And in the very next pew
a single mother of two
She takes my clothes at the
    cleaners and we'll
        talk for a few
And the couple I've seen at the
    bar drinking beer
God, I know I'm misplaced
    but what are they
        doing here?

Then the preacher interrupted,
    reading something from John
I never could find which
    page it was on
so I faked it quite casually
    and played like I was
        reading along
there were numbers -
    a 6 and 18
and a thus and a thine
    but I still think
        I know what it means

It seems I've been fearing all
    the wrong things

I felt a bit lighter
My shoulders relaxed
and I had a strange idea
   that I might just come back
I'll find my mom's bible
   somewhere on the shelf
and spend another hour next
   week not just
      thinking of myself

Jaundice

Grab a bottle of soda and drink
  it half full
Top it with vodka then take a
  long pull
It's a covert concoction
  to keep calm in the chaos
Liquidate your losses
Let your mind feel the pay off

And at family gatherings when
  there's a chill in the air
wine spritzers work quicker
  with a splash of Everclear

The recipe's simple
You get the picture
Any fluid in front of you
  serves as a mixer

Seagram's in your coffee
Tanqueray in your tea
Trembling hands on the table
  and a flask on your knee

But Sir Windsor is waning
He's fickle when he fades
And the Captain in your cola
casts a steely-eyed gaze

Trembles yield to shakes
Shakes devoured by seizures
And when the ambulance comes
the neighbors stare at your
    features
Oh, this stealth liquored life
    is full of surprises
Puzzled family members ask
    how you got hepatitis

It wasn't your intent
    to be so misleading
but the truth spurts out
    when there's
        internal bleeding

These secret libations
    gave your mind a vacation

But your liver stayed home
Worked itself to the bone

Now We're Free
(For Lisa)

My cautious heart
I encased it in galvanized steel
it beat in a place
   where it echoed
but didn't quite feel
you came along with a smile
   and a song
just in time
you stole it, then held it
   up close
like you would a small child

Your precious heart
split in parts
from earlier days
so you painted the cracks
with your colors
then went your own way
it's not a crime
but you're still doing time
patiently
then love turned your key
it's the same one for me
now we're free

now we're free

Plastic Virgins Die in the Shadows of Skyscrapers

Congratulations on your
  credit score
It appears you're quite a
  reliable Wall Street
    revenue source
"Top notch at generating
  income"
Just like the quote
  on my report

So you bought the lie too
It really isn't that hard
Did you pay for it
  the way I did
and put it on
  one of your cards?

I remember going plastic
I wasn't immune
I ended up paying 512 dollars
    for a pair of running shoes
I had a 60-inch Hi-def in my
    garage apartment
Cash I had little
but those shiny cards -
    what an assortment

I developed a leg palsy
    and a sore hip socket
From the 4 pounds of plastic
    I had filed in my pockets
but it was when I was limping
    that I finally got it-

An aura - like the glossy sheen
   of a platinum card
The interest pays Wall Street
   execs to live
      like rock stars-
Opulent second homes juxtaposed
   on private golf courses,
island trips, suctioned hips,
   and convertible Porsches

I quit swiping so much
   and slowly climbed
      out of the hole
But they were standing around it
   and they still won't
      leave me alone

So now when I take my ten
   dollars to buy a cap
      for my head
and the sales associate asks,
   "would you like to sign up
      for more debt?"
I politely say no
cordially decline
pay for my cap
   and then exit the line

But they follow you
ask on the street and online
and they'll ask in your doorway
   if you don't post a sign

So now I'll ask a question
as civilized as I can
What part of "back off
   motherfucker"
      don't you understand?

Hitting Home

Oh look at the pretty
  chem trail rings
from the circling jets
  on the tv screen
The attractive announcer
  on the evening news
says they're over us now
  and it's our turn soon

Well, I thought bombs fell
  in other places.
We see the images
  then send donations.
It's the cross we bear
  for other nations.
(But far away,
  not my location.)

They put webcams in the
    bomb bay doors,
so you can see them drop
    right from the source.
A real-time look as they
    surrealistically fall
on the military target - oh
    wait, that's a shopping mall.
And see the arcing rockets
    guided from afar.
"Look mommy, it's a
    falling star!"

When you're dodging bombs
    you're all alone,
with an analogue heart and a
    dead cell phone.

These pockets of diamonds?
They're weighing you down.

These leaders who lead us?
They live underground.

This New Exciting Information Age

Hey you—
in your cubicle,
ergonomic at your monitor,
aren't you glad you're part of
    this new exciting
        information age?!

For it wasn't long ago
you'd have to go out
    in the cold.
Walk through a park,
sometimes in snow.
Across a bridge
    of gothic stone,
to a building worn and old.

The librarian,
she is lovely.
Her smile could stop time.
And the smell of books,
the sound they make
when closed on a
    big oak table...

But hooray!!!!!!!!
That inefficient time is just
    a space on your
        mind's hard drive.
For you are part of this new
    exciting information age!

Data streams above the land.
While the corporate cloud
    rains down the same plan-
Make more money for the man.
With his executive suntan,
and his shoes
    shipped from Milan.

Selling your soul is so much
    faster using binary code.

Hey you-
sitting at your screen.
Wouldn't life be more serene
if you worked at Dairy Queen?

Humility Soldiers

Cinder block feet and
    cast iron legs
another morning struggling
    to get out of bed.
This depression's too big
    for a little blue pill.
The remedy I need
    a druggist can't fill.

Start with a run!
Then stopped at the end
    of the block.
(Well, it seemed like a good
    place to go for a walk.)
I knew this would be hard
    but it's proving much harder.
Well, tomorrow I'll run just a
    little bit farther.

And I found that phone number
    that I hid out of place,
and finally talked to someone
    with a similar faith.
A hundred dollars to sit in
    the therapy chair,
and all I could remember was
    to start with a prayer.

So I went home and I
    took the advice.
"God, why have I made such a
    mess of my life?"
No answer - not a whisper
    or shout.
Days later I heard,
    "I'm the only way out."

And how many times did I
    hear someone say
"Take care of yourself"
    well, how fucking cliché

But I did.

More running.
Less drinking.
Even spiritual reading.
And at night I began actually
    sleeping.
(not all through the night
    but this score
        I'm not keeping).

Then came the first sign
    I was starting to win-
I heard myself singing to my
    two dogs again.

And I kept going back to sit
    in that chair,
and started to realize it's not
    just me there.
These humans, the ones that
    God had called,
when my mind was racing
    and my heart had stalled,
they picked me up
    and pushed me out of the fog.

Now I just use them, these
    soldiers strong,
and hope they can use me before
    too long.

Western Girl

So you're leaving on wings
About to set sail
Fastened your case
and said your farewells

Well, don't forget to stop
    at the end of the block
and say goodbye to the kid
    who watched you grow up

There's not much left in this
    little old town
The fading letters on the
    water tower
The gas station that doesn't
    take credit cards
The swings sitting still in
    the old school yard

So take the county road
    to where the asphalt ends
on the highway past the cemetery
    where we'd share cigarettes
We read every tombstone
    that hot August night
then you danced young and free
    in the beam of car lights

Small towns aren't made for
    certain people it seems
The ones who can't breathe
    suffocated by dreams

The truckstop on the interstate
    lights up the train tracks
And I don't know
    where she's going
but I know she's not coming back

Dream Home

I live in a house with walls
    moving on hinges
They bend and they fold
    while I search for
        my children

The oldest girl's sick
delirium dreams in her head
and I crawl and I climb
but I can't reach her bed

The boy's in the garage
locked inside my old jeep
I see his face in the
    dash lights
his eyes begging for sleep

I'm racing in circles
I can't find the keys
Then I squeeze down the
    dark hallway
on my hands and my knees

The youngest girl's gone
Stuffed animals lie on her floor
Then wet footprints,
   dead light bulbs
and a wide open back door

I wake up in a sweat!
You can't sleep when you're cold
I put a towel on my pillow
and I change my wet clothes

Then I fall into a home that's
   damp and it's old
The windows won't shut and the
   doors won't stay closed
The wind, it keeps blowing
I can't keep my papers together
and the sky is the roof
so I'm wet from the weather

I live with an old man
    or does he live with me?
He's distant and sullen
doesn't speak, only breathes
I lay in the loft
Can you dream in a dream?
Sleepwalk to the mirror
The old man stares back at me

That's it
I've had it
I'm not sleeping at all!

Then I drift back again and
    find myself on a lawn
of a lovely dream dwelling,
    sturdy and calm
with an old English garden
    and ducks on a pond
I hear laughter and singing
    and the bark of a dog
These sounds keep me sleeping
and to a window I'm drawn

I see a thousand closed doors
    down a long spartan hall
and I'm not waking up
    until I've opened them all

Between the Wars

It's business as usual
The same ideas being sold
Save for the mothers
whose sons won't grow old
A thousand deaths
they'll suffer alone
All for the boy
who'll never come home

Idealism kills children
I don't understand it
But it seems middle-aged men
are the ones who have planned it
Sitting around a table
bloated and stuffed
protecting their assets
and acting so tough

So let's change the draft
"after 50 all a soldier!"
(then perhaps the negotiations
will last a little bit longer)
I'm sorry mr senator
I don't mean to sound terse
I'm willing to die for my country
but you can go first

Rope Burns

They taught us how to
    hold on tight
Then learn the ropes
    to ease the fight
Now I'm learning to
    just let it go
And take the fall
    to what's below

You've tied yourself
    in little knots
then fashioned a noose
    with the rope you've got
You didn't realize
    it would be so long
wrapped around all the ones
    you've strung along

Well, I've strung a bridge
It sways in the wind
And when I cross,
    I'll reel it in
A cowboy rising from the dust
I've looped a lasso and saddled up
I'll take the trailhead
    towards the sun
through a canopy of trees,
    then sky above

You've wrangled yourself
    so you can't move
Well, I'm moving on -
    these tracks are proof
My rope is strong
    from all its threads
Reminders I won't go back again

Seventies Man

Seventies man, oh, seventies man
The length of your sideburns
The depth of your tan
You are dominant
    yet sensitive male
dressed in stylish elephant bell

Out on a date with eighties girl
Your decade was empty when
    hers spilled into your world
A vision, with padded shoulders
    and towering hair
And you can't imagine breathing
    if she's not sitting there

A blissful union, at least at
    its inception
Dancing to The Flock of Seagulls
    at your wedding reception
Then a mortgage and babies
    and cars to afford
It's early to work and home late
    in your four-door Accord

But Nineties couple - they've
   got it all figured out
And with the stock market
   soaring is there
      even a doubt
Divide and prosper - that's
   the name of the game
But you're playing alone
   and the rules are deranged
and the kids are growing up
   forging lives of their own
Dark thoughts are noisy
   when it's quiet at home

Passenger jets fly into tall
   shiny buildings
A horror for most but for you
   the same feeling
So it's trendy drinks
   at Applebees-
it takes several to get drunk
and now your 401Ks in the
   gutter and your wife's
      in a funk

Do you sit as a couple
   on the therapy couch
Look deep into each other
Try to figure this out?
No, she's starting all over
   with a new younger spouse

Post-millennial middle-aged ghost
Your family can't see you when
    you need them the most
Transparent on the sofa with
    your dogs and dead hopes
Do you breathe carbon monoxide
    or swing from a rope?

Truth is so stealth
it hides in the stillness
Life is a gift not a terminal
    illness

and Grace is a gift too, not
    an earned earthly prize
so don't pick up the pieces
Simplify and downsize

Then helping each other's
    no longer a hassle
And your one-bedroom apartment
    feels like a castle

Sixties child, innocent faith
   bringing joy
Seventies man has grown up
   into a boy

With gratitude
to Mary Schwaner
at Prairie Muse Books

www.ingramcontent.com/pod-product-compliance
Lightning Source LLC
Chambersburg PA
CBHW051728050726
47598CB00003B/1089